SERIES EDITORS

JoAnn (Jodi) Crandall

Joan Kang Shin

AUTHORS

Kate Cory-Wright

Ronald Scro

Australia • Brazil • Japan • Korea • Mexico • Singapore • Spain • United Kingdom • United States

Let's sing! TR: B42

This is our world.
Everybody's got a song to sing.
Each boy and girl.
This is our world!

I say "our."
You say "world."
Our! World!
Our! World!

I say "boy."
You say "girl."
Boy! Girl!
Boy! Girl!

I say "Everybody move..."
I say "Everybody stop..."
Everybody stop!

This is our world.
Everybody's got a song to sing.
Each boy and girl.
This is our world!

Ha Long Bay, Vietnam

Unit 1	Wonders of the Sea	4
Unit 2	Good Idea!	14
Unit 3	That's Really Interesting!	24
Unit 4	The Science of Fun	34

Units 1-4 Review 44

Let's Talk Wow, that's cool! 46
            What does that mean? 47

Unit 5	Extreme Weather	48
Unit 6	Copycat Animals	58
Unit 7	Music in Our World	68
Unit 8	Life Out There	78

Units 5-8 Review 88

Let's Talk It's my turn 90
            Who's going to take notes? 91

Irregular Verbs 92
Unit songs 93
Cutouts 97
Stickers

Unit 1
Wonders of the Sea

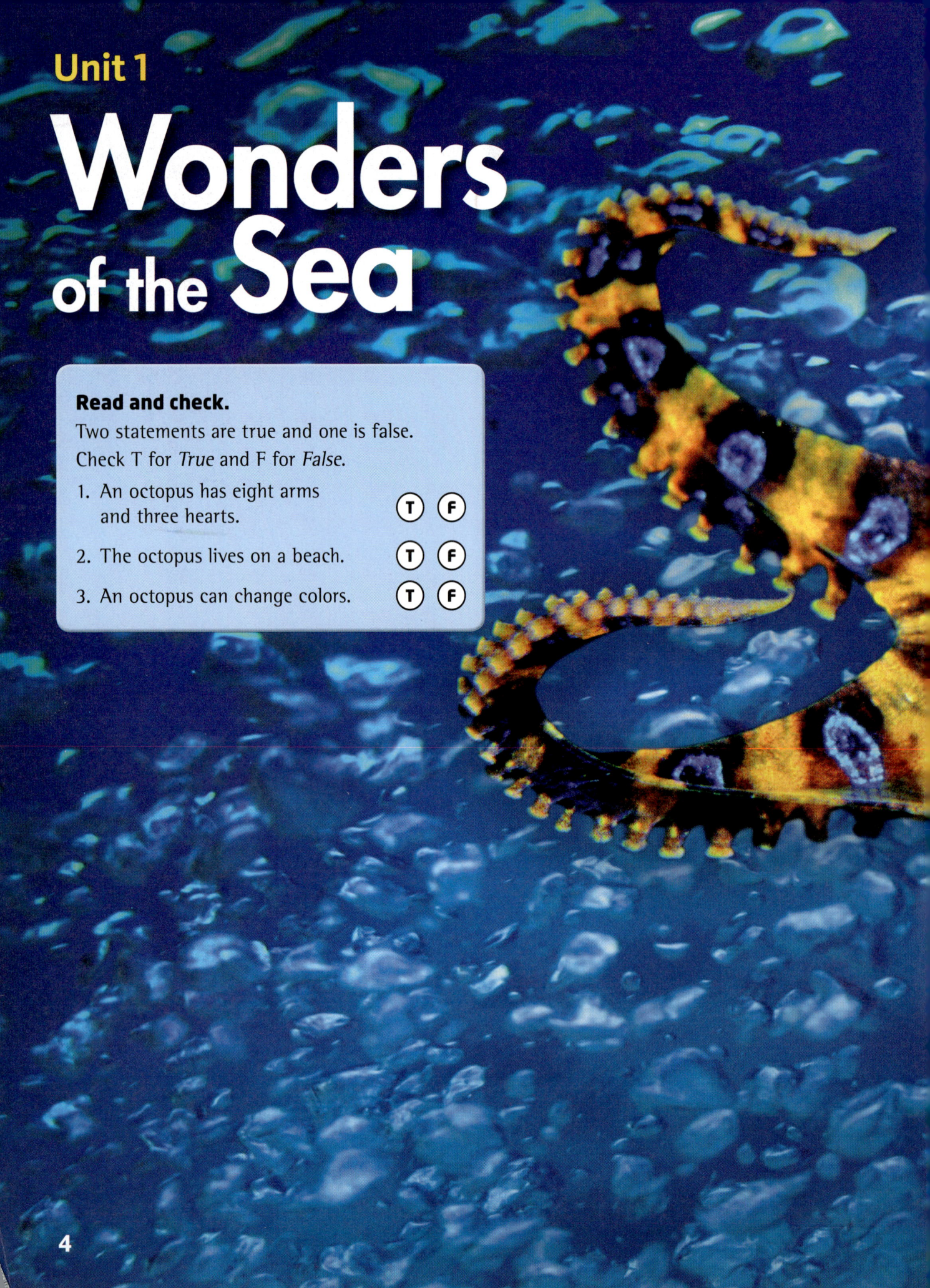

Read and check.
Two statements are true and one is false. Check T for *True* and F for *False*.

1. An octopus has eight arms and three hearts. T F
2. The octopus lives on a beach. T F
3. An octopus can change colors. T F

Blue-ringed octopus

1 **Listen and read.** TR: A2

2 **Listen and repeat.** TR: A3

We must protect the oceans and the seas because they are full of life. If we don't, these important **resources** will **disappear**.

Many animals live near the top of the ocean because they like the light. There is lots of food there, too. This part of the ocean is called the "sunlit zone." It goes down to about 137 m (450 ft.). **Dolphins** live here.

a whale

The middle **layer** of the ocean is called the "twilight zone." This is because there isn't much light. It goes down to about 1,000 m (3,300 ft.). Few animals live in this layer, but one that does live here is the **octopus**.

a squid

The bottom layer of the ocean is cold and black. It is called the "midnight zone" because the sun doesn't reach below 1,000 m (3,300 ft.). Some amazing animals live in this dark part of the ocean!

GRAMMAR TR: A4

We **have to** keep the oceans clean.
We **must** protect the oceans.

You **can't** throw trash into the ocean.
Don't leave food on the beach.

4 **Check.** Right or wrong?

	Right	Wrong
1. We must throw bags in the ocean.		✓
2. Don't leave trash in the classroom.		
3. At home, we have to go to bed late.		
4. In many schools, students can't use cell phones in class.		

5 **Work in groups of three.** Take turns. Talk about rules at home and at school. Use ideas and words from the list.

clean up (must)	use cell phones (can't)	go to bed (have to)	play loud music (don't)
shout (don't)	throw trash (can't)	help with chores (have to)	arrive on time (must)
help the teacher (must)	wash the dishes (have to)	raise your hand (have to / must)	talk (can't / don't)

Let's talk about rules at home.

We must clean up at home.

6 Listen and repeat. Then read and write. TR: A5

oil spill   garbage   pollution

plastic bags
not biodegradable

a paper bag
biodegradable

1. Oil spills, garbage, and dirty air are examples of ___pollution___.

2. Banana peels, plastic bottles, soda cans, old newspapers, boxes, and broken toys are examples of _____.

3. Big ships called tankers transport oil across the ocean. When they have an accident and oil escapes, the result is an _____.

4. Paper is _____. With time, it disappears.

5. _____ bottles and bags are not biodegradable.

7 Work with a partner. Listen, talk, and stick. TR: A6

> Oil spills happen when tankers have accidents on the ocean.

> You're right!

1   2   3   4   5

9

GRAMMAR TR: A7

What **will** happen in the future? Sea animals and plants **will** disappear.
We **won't** have clean air to breathe.

8 **Play a game with a partner.** Cut out the cards on page 97. Place them facedown in a pile. Ask and answer the questions, using *will* or *won't*.

Heads = 1 space   **Tails =** 2 spaces

START ... FINISH

You escaped!

— What will happen to the plastic bag?
— It won't disappear. It will stay in the sea.

10

9 **Listen, read, and sing.** TR: A8

Protect the Seas

*Please, please protect the seas.
Put good deeds into motion.
Help save the oceans.*

*We must protect
the wonders of the seas,
to make a better world
for you and me.*

*We must stop polluting
the ocean blue.
An octopus would like that,
and so would you.*

Humpback whale, Alaska, USA

THE SOUNDS OF ENGLISH TR: A9

sh**ar**k

10 **Listen and say.** Listen for the underlined sound. Then say the word.

1. st<u>ar</u>
2. sh<u>ar</u>k
3. l<u>ar</u>ge
4. g<u>ar</u>bage
5. movie st<u>ar</u>
6. guit<u>ar</u>

11 **Listen and read.** TR: A10

Colorful Corals

Corals look like a colorful garden under the water. But corals are not plants! They're animals.

What's for dinner? Each coral is made up of small animals called polyps. Polyps have a mouth, stomach, and tentacles to catch food. Many polyps live in the sunlit zone, where they eat small plants called algae.

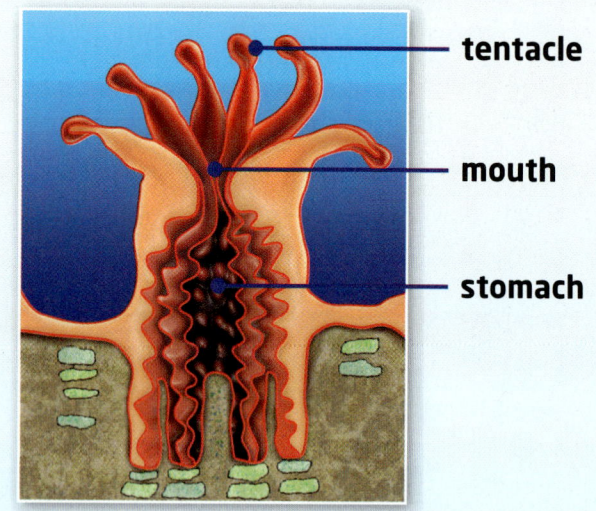
— tentacle
— mouth
— stomach

What's a coral reef? Most corals live together. As old corals die, new polyps grow on top. That's how you get a coral reef. Some coral reefs are millions of years old, and they're home to more than 4,000 kinds of fish!

Save the reefs! Coral reefs are amazing resources. They're important for tourism and jobs. Scientists use reef animals to make new medicines and other products. Coral reefs are a source of food, too. But coral reefs are in danger. Because of pollution, many coral reefs are disappearing. Some people say that only 30 percent of the world's corals will exist in the year 2050. We must protect our corals now.

The Great Barrier Reef is over 2,250 km (1,400 mi) long! You can see it from outer space!

12 **Work with a partner.** What did you learn? Ask and answer.

Protect the oceans.

Why must we protect the oceans?

Sylvia Earle diving, Honduras

Sylvia Earle
Oceanographer
Explorer-in-Residence

"With every drop of water you drink, every breath you take, you're connected to the ocean. No matter where on Earth you live. Taking care of the ocean means taking care of us."

Unit 2
Good Idea!

Look and check. Then answer the questions.

1. This is
   - ○ a rocket.
   - ○ an airplane.
   - ○ a train.
2. What kind of transportation do you use?
3. What kind of transportation would you like to try?

Shinkansen bullet train, Shinjuku, Japan

1 **Listen and read.** TR: A11

2 **Listen and repeat.** TR: A12

Inventions are everywhere. Look around you. What inventions can you see?

Five thousand years ago, people had a **problem.** They couldn't move big or heavy things! Then someone found the **solution**—the **wheel.** It changed our lives.

Imagine your life without electric lights. Before electricity, we didn't have **useful** things such as batteries, computers, and cell phones.

electricity

a battery

a wheel

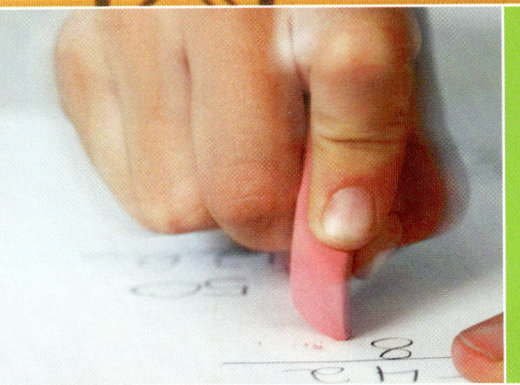

Inventors need **imagination.** Before the eraser, people used bread to erase writing! In 1839 Charles Goodyear had an **idea.** He **invented** the modern eraser.

The Wright brothers **tried** to fly many times, but they **failed.** Finally, in 1903, they **succeeded.** Now that we have planes, our world is very different.

3 **Work with a partner.** What did you learn? Ask and answer.

When did the Wright brothers fly a plane?

They flew a plane in 1903.

GRAMMAR TR: A13

People **used to** erase writing with bread.
Why **did** people **use to** read by candlelight?

We **didn't use to** have erasers.
They **didn't use to** have electric lights.

> did   didn't   used to   use to

4 **Complete the sentences.** Use words from the box. Then role play the conversation with a partner.

A: "_____ you _____ (make) phone calls when you were a kid, Dad?"

B: "Yes, I did. But I _____ (not / have) a cell phone."

A: "Really? So how _____ you _____ (text) your friends?"

B: "When I was young, we _____ (not / text) our friends.

We _____ (write) letters."

5 **Play tic tac toe.** Cut out the game board and cards on page 99. Talk about inventions.

Before we had electric lights, we used to use candles to read at night.

That's right! Mark a square with an *X*. My turn.

6 Listen and repeat. TR: A14

Complete. Then listen and check your answers. TR: A15

turn

lift

move

use

The "hula hoop" is an old invention, but it's very popular today. It's fun and it's good exercise!

1. How do you _____ a hula hoop? It's easy. Follow these instructions.

2. _____ the hula hoop on the ground. Stand in the middle.

3. _____ the hoop to your waist.

4. _____ your waist in a circle. Don't hold the hoop!

5. The hoop _____ around and around. Can you feel it?

7 Listen and stick. Put the stickers in order. Then tell your partner how to use this toy. Use the stickers to help you remember! TR: A16

1   2   3   4   5

GRAMMAR TR: A17

You need to have imagination to invent things.
What do **you** do with this invention?

You should always try again if **you** fail.
Do **you** play with it?

8 **Play a game.** Work with a partner. Ask questions about the inventions you see. Take turns.

Heads = 1 space   **Tails =** 2 spaces

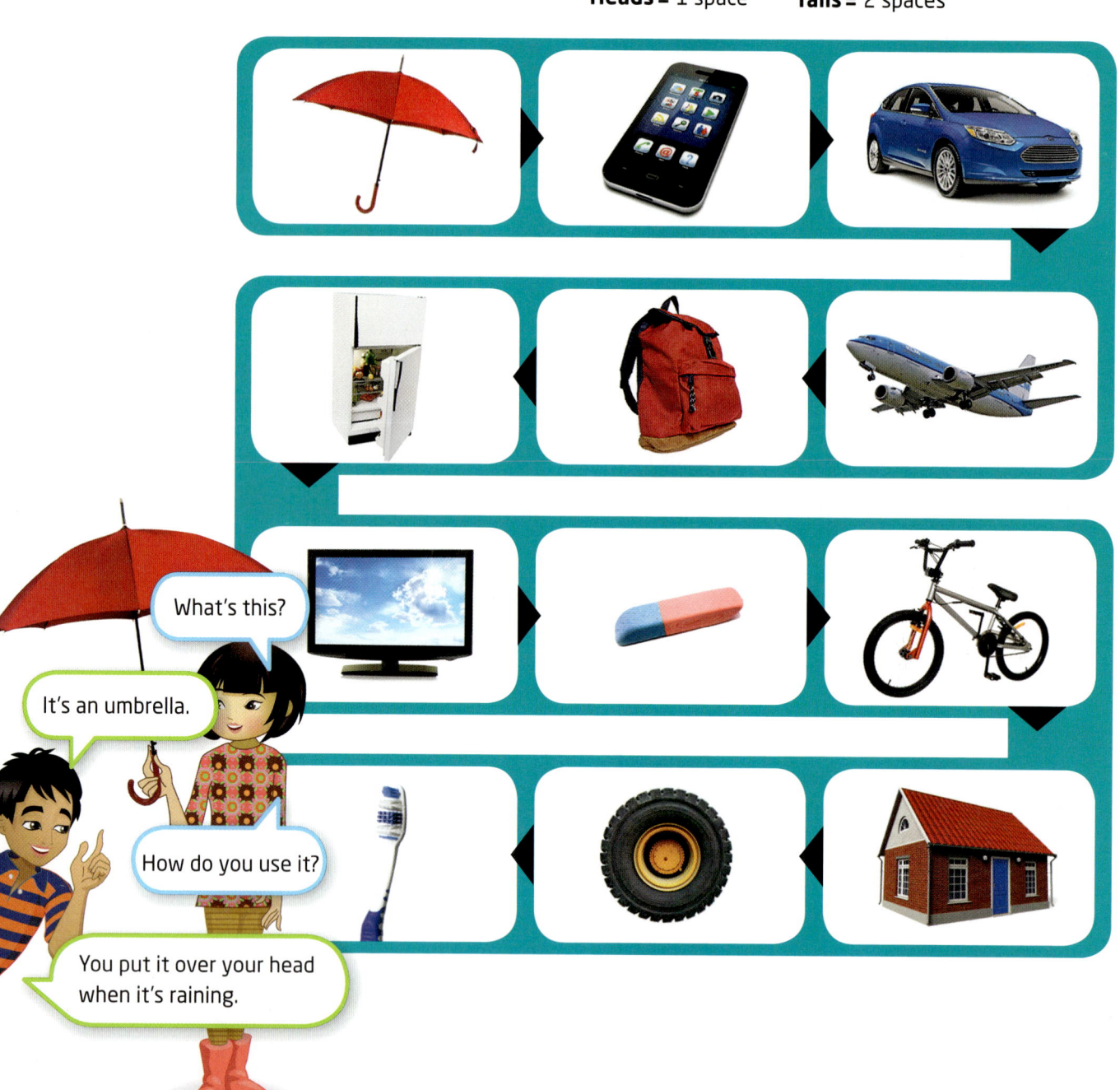

What's this?
It's an umbrella.
How do you use it?
You put it over your head when it's raining.

9 Listen, read, and sing. TR: A18

Inventions

Creativity!
Electricity!
Creativity changes the world!

Inventions solve problems.
Problems that we used to have are gone!
The wheel and the cell phone
help to make our world go around!

THE SOUNDS OF ENGLISH TR: A19

yes

10 Listen to the underlined sounds. Say the words.

1. year   you
2. yellow   use
3. useful   used to

11 Listen and read. TR: A20

Creative Kids

Did you know that a teenager had the first idea for a television? And a six-year-old boy invented the toy truck? Kids are great inventors because they have a lot of imagination.

1994: Chris Haas was nine years old when he designed a **"hands-on basketball."** His basketball has painted hands on it. The hands show you where to put *your* hands when you throw the ball. Today people all over the world use his invention.

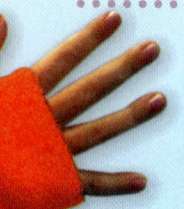

1994: **"Wristies"** protect you from the cold. Kathryn Gregory was only ten when she had the idea. She was in the snow and her wrists hurt because they were cold and wet. So she invented Wristies.

1905: When Frank Epperson was eleven, he left a cup with soda and a stick in his yard. That night he forgot about it. It was a very cold night. When he went outside the next morning he found something amazing: a **"Popsicle"**!

12 Work in groups of three. Discuss the questions. Do you have the same opinion?

Which story was the most interesting? Why?

Which invention was the most useful? Why?

NUMBER OF PATENT FILINGS AROUND THE WORLD

Diane Bisson, a Canadian industrial designer, invented plates and bowls that you can eat!

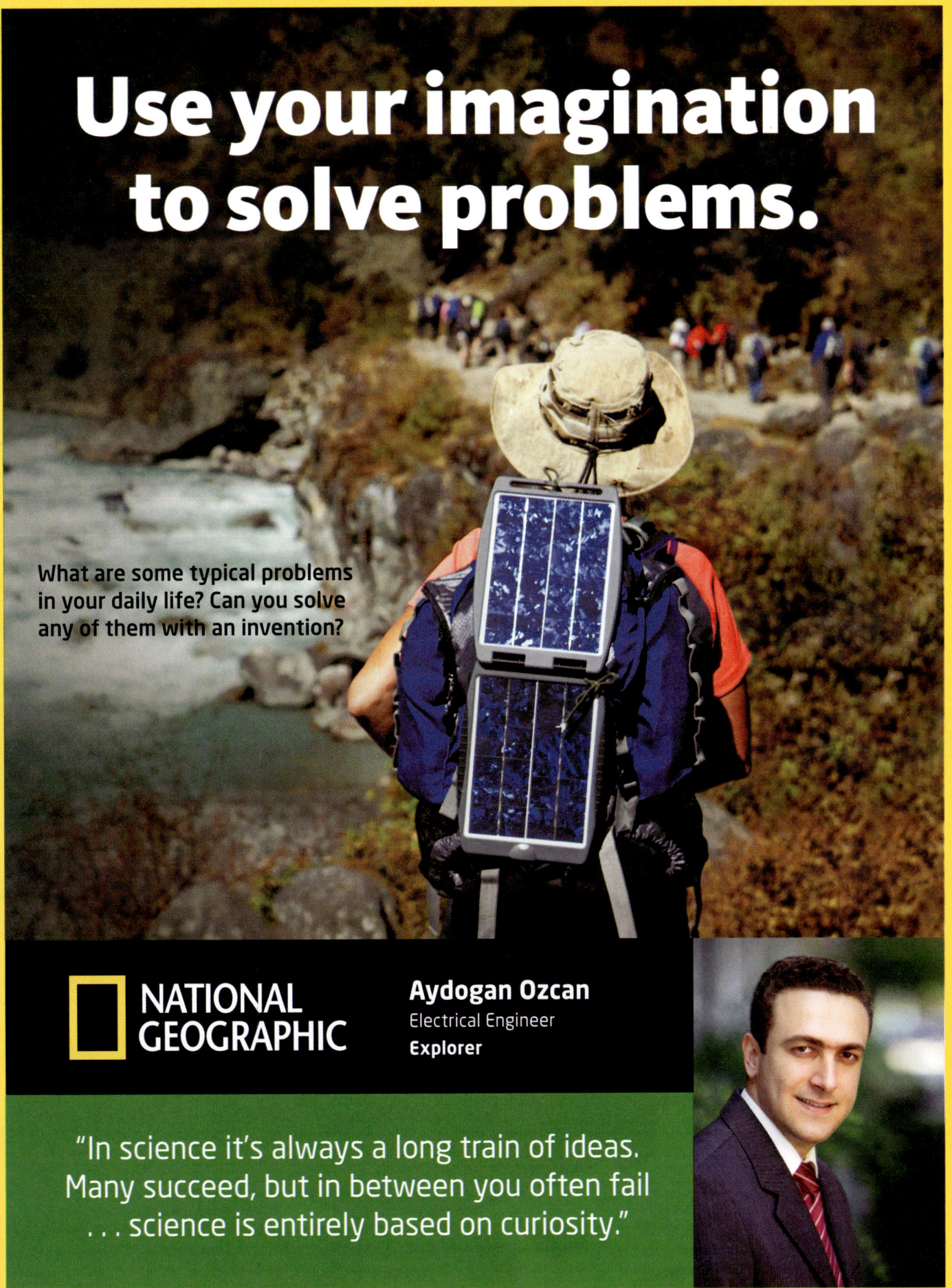

Unit 3

That's Really Interesting!

Look and check.

This person is
- ◯ feeding a pet.
- ◯ swimming with a whale.
- ◯ fishing.

The person is in
- ◯ the ocean.
- ◯ a river.
- ◯ a swimming pool.

Would you like to swim with a whale?

Diver and southern right whale, New Zealand

1. **Listen and read.** TR: A21

2. **Listen and repeat.** TR: A22

Most people have a hobby. Some children **collect** things, play music, or grow vegetables. Creative people paint or **take photos.** Video games are popular, too.

take photos

collect

Many video games are for one person. You play **alone.** But it's more fun to play with a friend. Choose your **avatars.** Then **compete.** To win the game, you must get the highest **score.**

In other video games, you play **together** with a friend. You don't compete. When you use the **controllers,** you can see your avatars move on the **screen.**

What hobbies do you **enjoy?**

GRAMMAR TR: A23

The person **who** has the highest score wins the game.
My friend **who** collects DVDs knows a lot about movies.

4 **Work in a group.** Ask questions. Write names. Then write about the people in your group.

Who . . .	Name(s)
1. enjoys reading books?	
2. likes to compete in sports?	
3. likes to play video games?	
4. is interested in fossils?	
5. collects something?	

Sofia is someone who enjoys reading books.

5 **Read and talk.** Work in a new group. Read some of your sentences. Don't read the name. Guess!

Trilobite fossil, Morocco

This person is someone who enjoys reading books. Who is it?

Is it Miguel?

No, it isn't. Try again!

6 **Listen and repeat.** Check **T** for *True* and **F** for *False*. TR: A24

a comic book

a bug

a fossil

a dinosaur

a stuffed animal

1. She's scared of bugs. T F
2. She thinks dinosaurs are boring. T F
3. She knows a boy who collects comic books. T F
4. Her brother collects fossils. T F
5. Her dad gave her a stuffed animal for her birthday. T F

7 **Work with a partner.** It's party time. What present would you like most? Stick. Ask and answer.

What gift would you like most?

I'd like a pair of socks.

Socks are boring! I'd like a fossil!

1   2   3   4   5

29

GRAMMAR TR: A25

My dad gave this fossil **to me**. = My dad gave **me** this fossil.

My mom bought stuffed animals **for them**. = My mom bought **them** stuffed animals.

Show the comic book **to James**. = Show **James** the comic book.

8 **Read and write.** Rewrite the sentences.

1. When my brother was in the hospital, my uncle gave a stuffed animal to him.

   When my brother was in the hospital, my uncle gave him a stuffed animal.

2. My cousin sent a dinosaur book to him.

   _____

3. He became friends with two kids and gave two comic books to them.

   _____

4. Grandma sent a present to him, and he wrote a letter to her.

   _____

9 **Play a game.** Cut out the game board and the cube on page 101. Work with a partner. Take turns.

My friend gave me a toy dinosaur!

Yes, he gave a toy dinosaur to me.

Really?

me = 1 space 😊

him/her/them = 0 spaces 😞

10 Listen, read, and sing. TR: A26

What's Your Hobby?

What's your hobby?
What do you like to do?
What's your hobby?
I have a hobby, too!

The boy who has the highest score
wins the video game.
The girl who collects a fossil
wants to learn its name.

THE SOUNDS OF ENGLISH TR: A27

b**oy**

11 Listen and say. Underline the words that have the sound that you hear in *boy*. How fast can you say the sentence?

The noisy boy enjoys stuffed toys.

12 Listen and read. TR: A28

Hide and Seek

"Letterboxing" is a fun outdoor hobby. Here's how it works: People hide a box. Inside the box, they put a rubber stamp and a notebook. They post clues on websites to help you find the box.

You look on the website and read the clues. Then you look for the letterbox! You need to have your Internet clues, a pen or pencil, a notebook, and a rubber stamp. You may need a compass, too.

When you find the letterbox, you look for the notebook inside. Then you write your name, your hometown, and the date. You press your rubber stamp on the page. Then you take the stamp from inside the box and stamp it in your notebook. Finally, you wrap the box carefully. You leave it where you found it for another person to find. Try it! You will enjoy it!

13 Write. Label the pictures.

a. ~~notebook~~   b. rubber stamp   c. clue   d. compass

"Keep your back to the tree and take four steps."

14 Work in a group. Discuss what people should take with them when they go letterboxing.

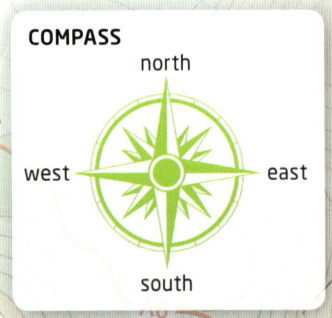

COMPASS — north, west, east, south

A Japanese sailor sent a message in a bottle when his boat was sinking. The message asked for help. About 150 years later, the bottle arrived in the town where he was born!

Unit 4

The Science of Fun

Look and answer.

1. Name some of the things you see in the photo.
2. What is the man doing?
3. What is the man thinking? Write a caption for the photo.

Chamonix, France

1 Listen and read. TR: A29

2 Listen and repeat. TR: A30

We use **force** to move. Force **happens** when we **push** or **pull.** Do you push or pull when you move on a swing? You do both.

Look at this **skater.** To move, skaters push on the ice. A push can move a skater **forward.** It can also move a skater **backward.**

forward

Skaters pull, too. Look at these skaters. The more one skater pulls, the more they **spin**. The skaters don't **fall over** because they know how to **balance**.

skaters

backward

3 **Work with a partner.** What did you learn? Ask and answer.

How do skaters move?

They push on the ice.

37

GRAMMAR TR: A31

The	more	she pushes,	the	higher	he goes.
The	higher	he goes,	the	more	he feels sick.
The	sicker	he feels,	the	worse	he looks!

4 Match the sentences to the pictures.

a   b   c

1. __c__ The more she pushes, the higher he goes.

2. _____ The harder he pulls, the faster they spin.

3. _____ The more he goes up, the more she comes down.

5 Look and write. Write a sentence about each person. Use the words in the box.

| more | higher | harder | faster | better | kick |
| push | get | spin | practice | go | |

The harder I push, the faster I go!

38

6 **Listen and repeat.** Read and write. Complete the sentences. TR: A32

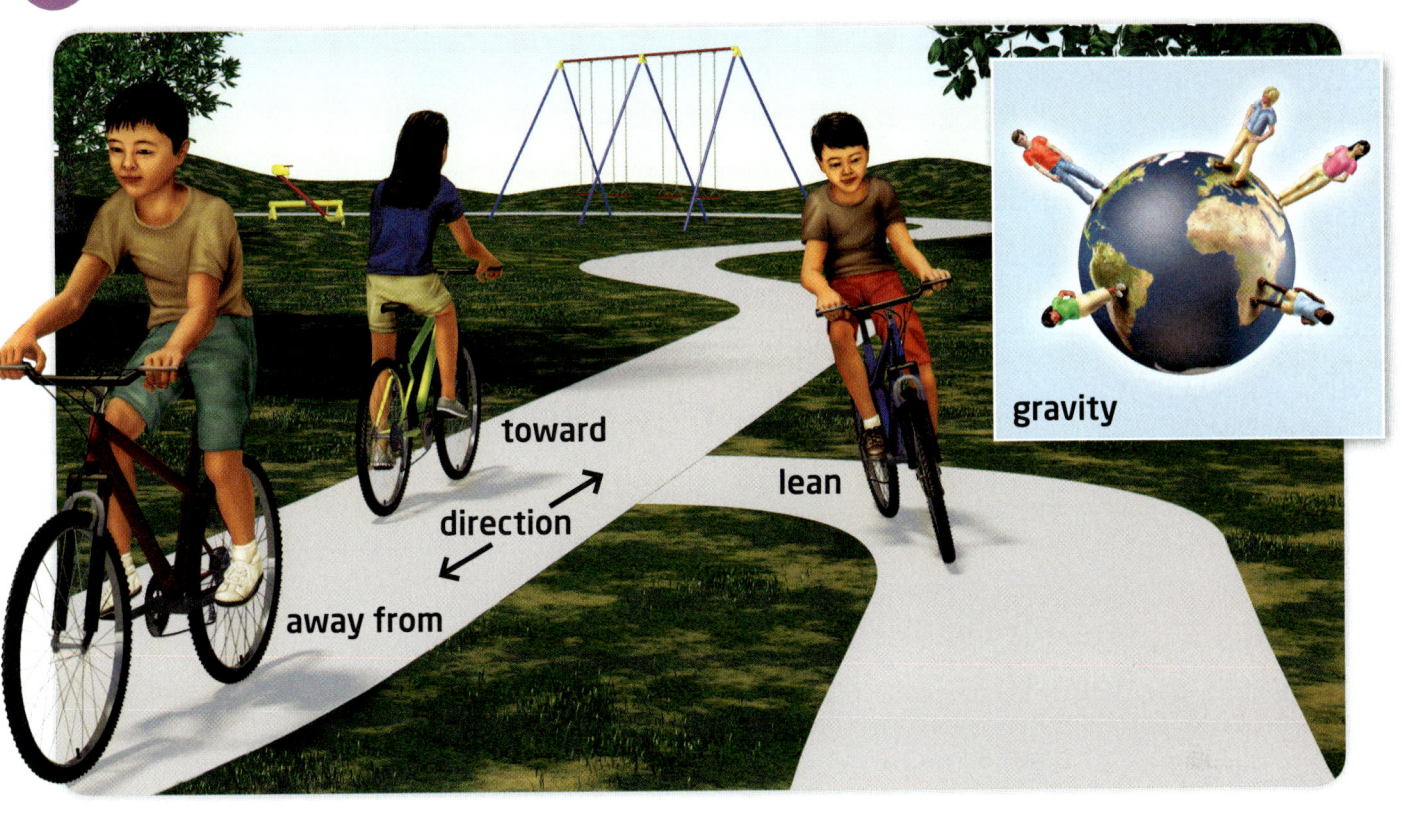

1. When you throw a ball, _____ pulls it toward the earth.
2. Don't go in that _____. Turn left!
3. He is walking _____ the music because it's too loud.
4. When you ride your bicycle and want to turn left, you turn your wheels to the left, and you _____ to the left.
5. She is riding _____ the swings because she wants to play on them.

7 **Listen and stick.** Work with a partner. Compare your answers. TR: A33

1 2 3 4 5

GRAMMAR TR: A34

The force **which** pulls you toward the center of the earth is called gravity.
Skates are special shoes **which** you wear when you go ice skating.

8 **Complete the definition for each item.** Work with a partner. Write in your notebook. Then read your definitions and guess. Take turns.

Example: bicycle: a machine _with wheels which you can ride in the park_.

skateboarding: a hobby _____

friction: a force _____

bingo: a game _____

soccer: a sport _____

9 **Play a game.** Play with a partner. Cut out the cards on page 103. Take turns.

= Pick up a card.

A bicycle is a machine with wheels and handlebars which you ride.

OK! My turn!

40

10 Listen, read, and sing. TR: A35

I'm on the Move!

Push it! Pull it! Push it! Pull it! Push! Pull!
Push! Pull! Push! Pull! Watch it go!

If you spin around, and around and
around and around,
what you feel is force.
If you fall down, down, down, down,
down to the ground,
that's gravity, of course.

I'm on the move.
I'm in the groove.
It's amazing what you can do
when you let force do the work for you!

THE SOUNDS OF ENGLISH TR: A36

p<u>u</u>sh

11 Listen to the underlined sounds.
Say the words.

1. p<u>u</u>sh   p<u>u</u>ll   p<u>u</u>t
2. t<u>oo</u>k   c<u>oo</u>k   f<u>oo</u>t
3. c<u>ou</u>ld   sh<u>ou</u>ld   w<u>ou</u>ld

12 Listen and read. TR: A37

Up, Down, and All Around!

You are going on a roller coaster ride. Sit in the car and pull down the safety bar. Are you ready? Let's go!

First, you go up a steep hill. The roller coaster goes slow. Suddenly, when you reach the top, the roller coaster goes down the hill very quickly. Gravity pulls you down. Whoooosh! You feel very light!

Next you reach a big circle, called the "loop-the-loop." This part is many people's favorite. First, you go up the circle, and you feel heavy. Gravity is pulling you down. Then you reach the top. You're high in the sky and you're hanging upside down! So why don't you fall out of your seat? Your body wants to fly off, but the speed of the car and a force called centripetal force keep you moving in a circle, and keep you in your seat!

The roller coaster uses friction to stop. If it stops quickly, your body wants to continue moving. But the safety bar keeps you in place! Roller coasters are the best!

13 Look and discuss. Work with a partner. Describe a ride on a roller coaster.

Weird but true

The Russians invented the roller coaster. They made the "cars" from ice. And they put fur on the seats to keep the passengers warm.

What does your favorite roller coaster look like?

It looks like a spaceship!

What happens first?

You go straight toward a moon, but then you turn!

Think creatively and critically.

Why is it important to understand how and why things work?

Spiral galaxy, photograph from Hubble Space Telescope

NATIONAL GEOGRAPHIC

Stephon Alexander
Theoretical Physicist
Emerging Explorer

"When something unexpected or unusual happens, I am always curious to find out why."

Review

1 Listen. Circle the inventions that you hear. TR: A38

airplane   plastic   eraser   wheel

2 Listen again. Answer the questions. TR: A39

1. What was Charles Goodyear's idea? _____

2. What is Anya's score at the end of the competition? _____

3. What will Anya do next month? _____

3 Work with a partner. Take turns. Ask and answer questions about life at school. Use the words in the boxes.

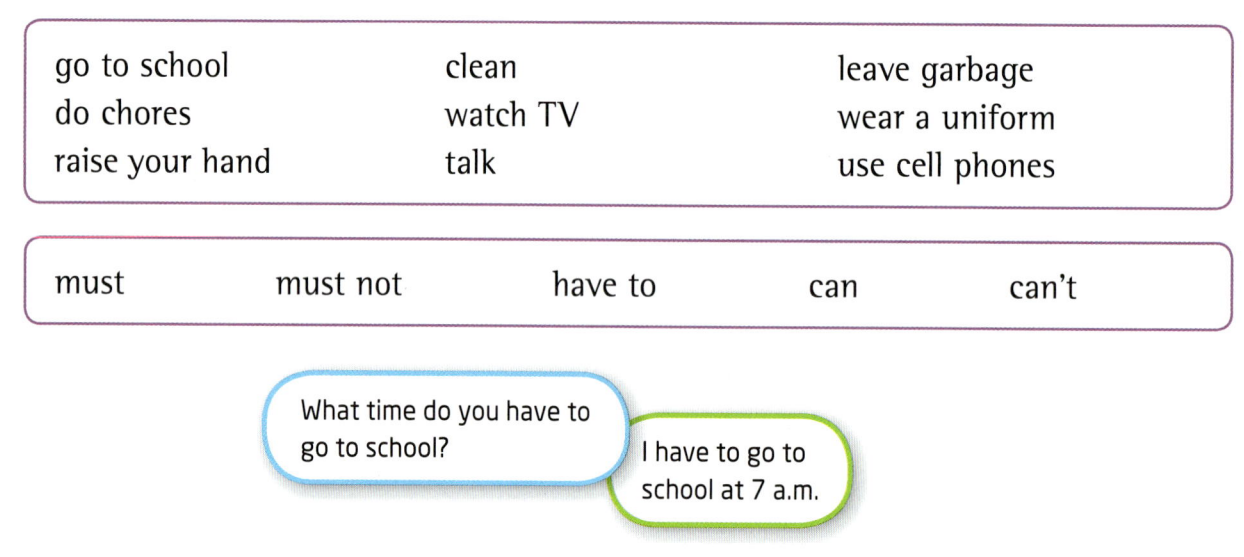

go to school	clean	leave garbage
do chores	watch TV	wear a uniform
raise your hand	talk	use cell phones

| must | must not | have to | can | can't |

> What time do you have to go to school?

> I have to go to school at 7 a.m.

4 Write. Make sentences about life before these inventions, using *used to*.

| computers | TV | the internet | airplanes | erasers |

Before computers, people used to spend more time together.

44

5 Read and write.

| a dinosaur | a solution | a hobby | an inventor |
| a skater | plastic | together | toward |

1. This is a person who moves, turns, and spins on ice. _____
2. Collecting fossils is an example of this. _____
3. This is a person who invents things. _____
4. This is a creature which lived millions of years ago. _____
5. It's the opposite of *alone*. _____
6. It's the opposite of *away from*. _____
7. It's the opposite of a problem. _____
8. Bags made from this are not biodegradable. _____

6 Work with a partner. Choose list A, B, or C. Write definitions in your notebook.

A
- an avatar
- an octopus
- a comic book
- a creative person
- (to) pull

B
- a bug
- a shark
- a good friend
- a problem
- a wheel

C
- biodegradable
- gravity
- a screen
- a stuffed animal
- (to) take photos

It's the opposite of push.

It's the force that pulls you toward the earth.

7 Work in a group. Take turns. Read your definitions to the group. Can they guess?

8 Work in a group. Make predictions about the world 40 years from now, using *will* and *won't*.

We won't go to movie theaters anymore.

Let's Talk

Wow, that's cool!

I will . . .
- ask questions.
- show I'm interested.
- keep the conversation going.

1 **Listen and read.** TR: A40

Pablo: What's your favorite sport?
Mario: Soccer. I want to be a professional soccer player.
Pablo: **Do you?**
Mario: Yeah! **What about you?** What's your favorite sport?
Pablo: I love soccer, too. My dad is taking me to the World Cup!
Mario: Wow. **That's so cool!**

Do you? (Can you? / Are you?) Really? Wow.	**What about you?** How about you? And you?	**That's so cool!** That's amazing. How cool!

2 **Work with a partner.** Use the chart. Talk about your favorite hobby or person.

What does that mean?

I will . . .
- interrupt someone (formally and informally).
- ask the meaning and ask how to spell or say something.
- explain a meaning and give a spelling.
- say that I don't know.

3 **Listen and read.** TR: A41

Antoni: **Hey,** Martina, **what does this mean?**
Martina: **I don't know. I think it's a kind of** weather.
Antoni: Um, I don't think so.
Martina: Why don't you ask the teacher?
Antoni: **That's a good idea. Excuse me,** Ms. Biga. What does this word mean?

Hey, Excuse me, Mr. / Ms. / Mrs. _____.	What does _____ mean?	I think it's a kind of _____. I think it means _____. It's the opposite of _____.	I don't know. I'm not sure.	That's a good idea. Good point.
	How do you spell _____? How do you pronounce this word? How do you say _____?			

4 **Listen.** You will hear two discussions. Read each question and circle the answer. TR: A42

1. What does the boy want to know?
   a. meaning   b. spelling   c. pronunciation

2. What does the girl want to know?
   a. meaning   b. spelling   c. pronunciation

5 **Work in pairs.** Prepare and practice discussions. You want to know the spelling, the meaning, or the pronunciation of a word. Ask your partner and then ask the teacher.

Unit 5

Extreme Weather

Look. Underline the correct word or words.

1. It's   hot.   warm.   freezing cold.

2. The person is   walking.   running.   ice skating.

Look and discuss.

3. Why do you think there is ice on the trees?

4. What's your favorite kind of weather?

Versoix, Switzerland

1 **Listen and read.** TR: B2

2 **Listen and repeat.** TR: B3

The weather is beautiful and dangerous at the same time. In a thunderstorm, you can hear loud **thunder** and see **lightning**. It's amazing to watch, but lightning is electricity! If lightning hits people, it can hurt them. People should stay away from trees and go indoors during a thunderstorm.

Wind is a dangerous force. The winds in a **tornado** move at a **speed** of 500 kilometers (300 miles) an hour. A **hurricane** is a powerful **storm** that can also move very fast, although the "eye" at the center is calm. Strong hurricanes can break windows, so people usually prepare by covering their windows. They also buy food and water because a hurricane can last over a week.

Rain is a strong force. When a lot of rain falls quickly, there can be a **flood**. If the flood is very bad, people **evacuate** their homes and go somewhere safe until the rain stops. It's always best to move away from extreme weather!

lightning

a hurricane

eye of the storm

a tornado

a sandstorm

a blizzard

a drought

3 **Work with a partner.** What did you learn? Ask and answer.

There's lightning! What should we do?

We should go inside.

51

GRAMMAR TR: B4

Is it **going to** rain tomorrow? No, it's **going to** snow tomorrow.
I'm **going to** listen to the weather report at 8:00.
He's **going to** put on his snow boots.

4 **Play a game.** Choose a day of the week. Ask your partner about the weather. Spin. Answer your partner's question.

5 **Work with a partner.** What are you going to do? Ask and answer.

1. It's going to rain tomorrow.
2. A blizzard is coming.
3. You can hear thunder. There's going to be lightning.
4. A big storm is coming. It's an emergency!

It's going to rain tomorrow.

I know! I'm going to take my umbrella to school.

6 Listen and repeat. Then read and write. TR: B5

an emergency

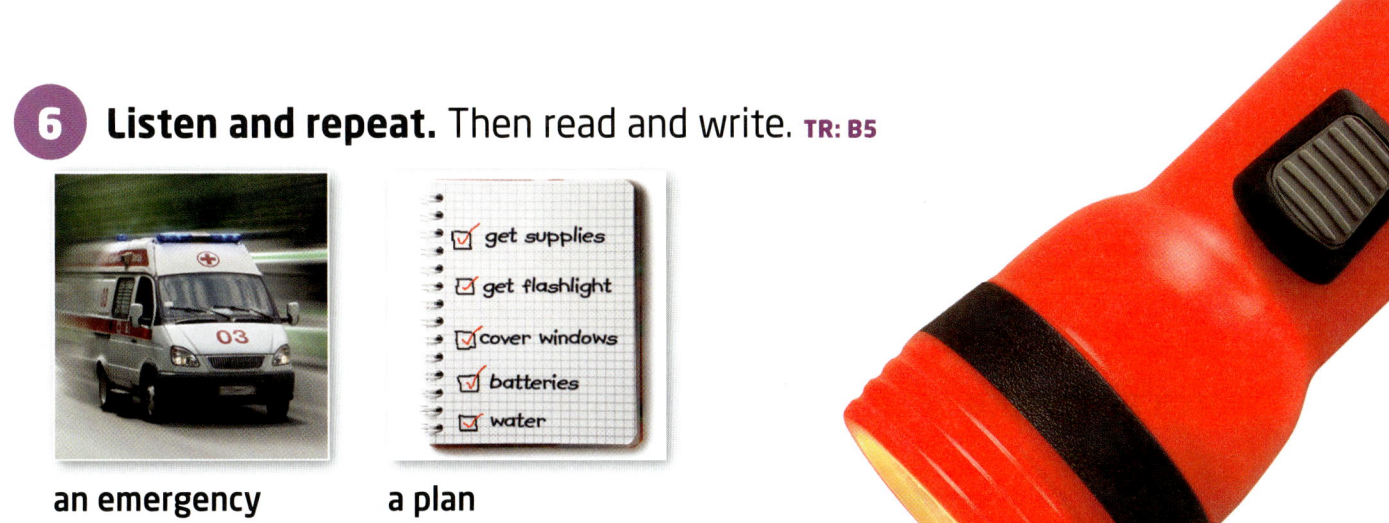

a plan

a flashlight

supplies

a shelter

When a weather forecaster predicts bad weather, you should make a _____. To protect yourself from bad weather, you can go to a _____. If the electricity goes off, use a _____ to see in the dark. You can store _____ in a safe place so that you have enough to eat. In an _____ like a hurricane, move quickly but stick to your plan.

7 Listen and stick. Find out what to do next. Place your stickers in the correct order. Work with a partner. TR: B6

A hurricane is coming. It's an emergency.

Yes, I put emergency in number 1. That's correct.

1   2   3   4   5

GRAMMAR TR: B7

If the weather **is** cold, **I put on** my winter coat.
If I **see** lightning, **I go** inside.
If a sandstorm **comes**, I **close** all the windows.

8 **Match and make logical sentences.** Work with a partner. Use *if*.

I see lightning when I'm swimming	I look for a boat
it rains	I wear gloves and boots
a storm comes	I try to stay cool
the temperature rises	get out of the water
a flood comes	go inside the house
it snows	I carry an umbrella

9 **Play a game.** Cut out the cards on page 105. Match and make sentences. Play with a partner.

If it rains, I use an umbrella.

10 Listen, read, and sing. TR: B8

Bad Weather

There's bad weather on the way!
There's bad weather on the way!

Is it going to storm? Yes, it is!
Is there going to be lightning? Yes, there is!
Is there going to be thunder? Yes, there is!

When there's going to be a storm, I hurry inside!

Be prepared for emergencies.
It's always good to be safe. You'll see!
Grab supplies and a flashlight, too.
Seek shelter. It's the safe thing to do!

THE SOUNDS OF ENGLISH TR: B9

wea**th**er

11 **Listen and say.** Pay attention to the sound of the underlined letters in each word. Can you hear the difference?

thanks	this
thunder	that
birthday	something

12 Listen and read. TR: B10

Tornado Trouble

Tornadoes happen all over the world. They are spinning columns of air that come from thunderstorms. The most dangerous tornadoes are very fast. In ten minutes they can break windows, lift trees, and throw cars into the air.

Josh Wurman is a scientist who studies tornadoes. He tries to predict them so that he and his team can save lives. One day Josh Wurman watched a tornado in Tornado Alley. It was amazing. First, the blue sky turned black. Then a big cloud came toward him and the team. The cloud had winds that moved in a circle. When the cloud touched the ground, it became a tornado.

Inside his truck, Wurman watched from a safe distance. The tornado twisted and turned for half an hour. It moved one way, then another way. It looked like a big, gray elephant's trunk. Then suddenly it leaned over like a soft rope. Poof! It was gone!

Weird but true: It once rained frogs on a town in Serbia. A small tornado dropped them there.

Step 1 Warm air and cold air come together.

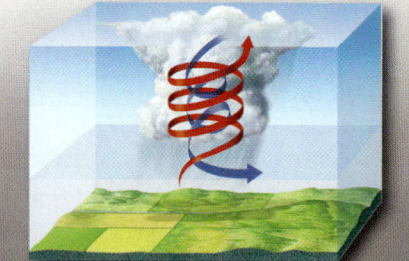

Step 2 The warm air moves up. The cold air moves down.

Step 3 The funnel of wind touches the ground.

13 Work in a small group. Discuss what you should do in a tornado. Use the ideas in the box to help you.

drive away from it	hide under a heavy table	sit next to a window
stay indoors for 10 minutes	help people	cover your head with your arms

If you're in a car and you see a tornado, you should drive away from it.

No way! You should get out of the car and lie down in a low-lying place on the ground.

Understand weather.

Why is it important to understand weather?

Storm chasers, Oklahoma, USA

NATIONAL GEOGRAPHIC

Tim Samaras
Severe Storm Researcher

"It all started when I was about six years old and saw that fantastic tornado in *The Wizard of Oz*."

Unit 6

Copycat Animals

Check T for *True* and F for *False*. Then answer the question.

1. This animal lives in the ocean. T F
2. It's a different color from the plants around it. T F
3. What do you think this animal eats?

Allied cowrie,
Papua New Guinea

1 **Listen and read.** TR: B11

2 **Listen and repeat.** TR: B12

Some animals can change how they look. They know how to look like other animals, or even like a plant! These copycats are trying to hide from a hungry **predator.** Sometimes they play tricks on the predator. They try to look like another more dangerous animal or like an animal the predator doesn't like to eat.

spots

a predator

This cheetah's black **spots** act as **camouflage.** This way, the cheetah doesn't scare its **prey** when it's time to **hunt.**

a stripe

This colorful frog has **stripes** on its skin. The bright colors tell hungry predators that the frog is **poisonous.**

prey

These butterflies are not the same **species**, but they look like each other. The top one tastes bad. The other one **copies** its shape and colors. It tastes bad, too!

This **insect** is as green as a leaf. It copies the color and shape of leaves so that predators think it is a leaf.

3 **Work with a partner.** What did you learn? Ask and answer.

How do some frogs show they are poisonous?

They have bright colors.

61

GRAMMAR TR: B13

That insect is **as green as** a leaf.
Some frogs are **as dangerous as** snakes.
This butterfly is **not as pretty as** the blue one.

4 **Play a game.** Cut out the cards on page 107. Choose an animal from each group and compare them. Use the words in the box.

fast   heavy   slow   loud
cool   cute   beautiful   ugly

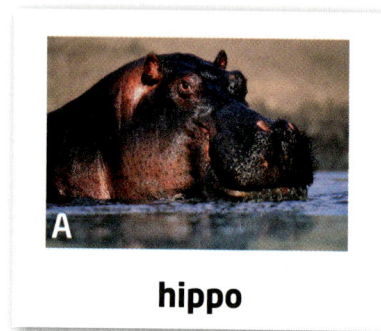

A **hippo**

B **elephant**

Hippos are as heavy as elephants.

And a hippo can run as fast as a person!

5 **Listen and repeat.** Then read and write. TR: B14

hide   attack / defend   escape

1. All predators _____ prey.

2. Many birds put their eggs in the ground or in a tree.

   They _____ their eggs from predators.

3. Animals always fight hard to _____ their babies and

   themselves against predators.

4. If a rabbit runs very fast, it can _____ from a bigger animal.

6 **Listen.** Stick *True* or *False*. Work with a partner.
Compare your answers. TR: B15

> The insect is the same color as the leaf. It's hiding. This is true.

> You're right! My turn.

1   2   3   4

63

GRAMMAR TR: B16

Lightning **is** dangerous, **isn't it?**
Sharks **are** scary, **aren't they?**
This insect **looks** like a stick, **doesn't it?**
Your friends **don't eat** meat, **do they?**

That frog **wasn't** poisonous, **was it?**
The boy **escaped** the dog, **didn't he?**
The dogs **were** loud, **weren't they?**
The cats **weren't** friendly, **were they?**

7 **Read.** Underline the correct answer.

1. It's very hot, doesn't it? / isn't it?

2. It was really hot yesterday, didn't it? / wasn't it?

3. Cats like sleeping in the sun, doesn't it? / don't they?

4. Baby penguins are so cute, aren't they? / weren't they?

5. That wasn't a bad movie, was it? / did it?

8 **Play a game.** Cut out the question tags on page 107. Choose nine and glue them to the grid. Then listen. If you have the tag, draw an *X* on the square. TR: B17

I have three in a row!

9 Listen, read, and sing. TR: B18

It's a Wild World

It's a wild world!
It's work to stay alive!
Animals do amazing things
in order to survive.

An insect that looks like a leaf
copies plants to get relief.
Predators are everywhere,
and looking for a feast!

THE SOUNDS OF ENGLISH TR: B19

cra**z**y

10 Listen and say the words. Pay attention to the sound of the underlined letter in each word.

1. <u>z</u>oo   <u>z</u>ebra

2. ama<u>z</u>ing   poi<u>s</u>onous

3. i<u>s</u>n't it   wa<u>s</u>n't it

Lionfish, Indonesia

11 **Listen and read.** TR: B20

The Copycat Dragon

The leafy sea dragon is a weird but beautiful copycat. From its name you'd think it's a kind of dragon, wouldn't you? But no, the leafy sea dragon gets its name from its funny shape.

The leafy sea dragon copies what's around it. It lives in seaweed, and so its body looks like a seaweed leaf. The sea dragon imitates the shape and color of seaweed, and it even looks like floating seaweed when it moves! It doesn't use the parts of its body that look like leaves to swim. It uses fins that are transparent, so it's hard to see them move.

The leafy sea dragon doesn't only look like a copycat. It also dances like a copycat. A male and female sea dragon will copy each other's movements for hours!

12 **Work with a partner.** Number the facts. Decide which fact is the most interesting (1) and the least interesting (4).

_____ Its name

_____ Its color and shape

_____ The tricks it plays on its prey

_____ How it moves and dances

Weird but true

One kind of spider tricks predators by imitating an ant. It holds two legs up to look more like an ant when it walks.

leafy sea dragon

I think the most interesting thing is its name.

I agree. It's not a dragon at all.

Protect biodiversity.

How are the species of animals in this unit different? Why is it important to preserve this diversity?

A tarsier

NATIONAL GEOGRAPHIC

Krithi Karanth
Conservation Biologist
Emerging Explorer

"We need to increase people's interest and awareness about wildlife and conservation issues and reduce the general disconnect from nature."

Unit 7
Music in Our World

Circle the correct answer.

1. The man is playing
   a. a piano.
   b. a drum.
2. The light is coming from
   a. the sun.
   b. the moon.

Discuss.
What musical instrument do you like? Why?

Makena Beach, Maui

1 **Listen and read.** TR: B21

2 **Listen and repeat.** TR: B22

There are three main types of musical instruments:

1. Wind instruments - To make music, you blow air through them with your mouth. The **saxophone** and the **flute** are wind instruments.

2. String instruments - They make music when you move the strings. The **guitar** and the **violin** are string instruments.

3. Percussion instruments - You hit or shake them. The **drum** is a percussion instrument. The *thump, thump, thump* of a percussion instrument makes the **beat.**

a guitar

a flute

a drum

Would you like to be in a **band?** You have to **practice** hard, but when your band sounds good, you can play for an audience. Invite your friends to the **concert!** If you don't play an instrument but you have a good voice, you could be the **lead singer!**

3 **Work with a partner.** What did you learn? Ask and answer.

How many types of instruments are there?

There are three main types.

GRAMMAR TR: B23

Have you **ever played** the piano?
Have you **ever danced** to this music?
Has Lisa **ever been** to a concert?
Has she **ever heard** the saxophone?

Yes, I **have.**
No, I **haven't.**
Yes, she **has.**
No, she **has never heard** it.

4 **Read.** Complete the sentences. Use *have* or *has*.

1. This song is new. I _____haven't heard_____ (not / hear) it before.

2. I _____ (never / go) to see an opera. I don't think I'd like it.

3. _____ (listen to) this band? Yes, I have.

4. My dad _____ (never / dance)!

5 **Play a game.** Use the game board on page 109. Play in a small group. Ask and answer.

Chinese opera

Have you ever gone to a concert?

Yes, I have. It was great.

6 Listen and repeat. Then read and write. TR: B24

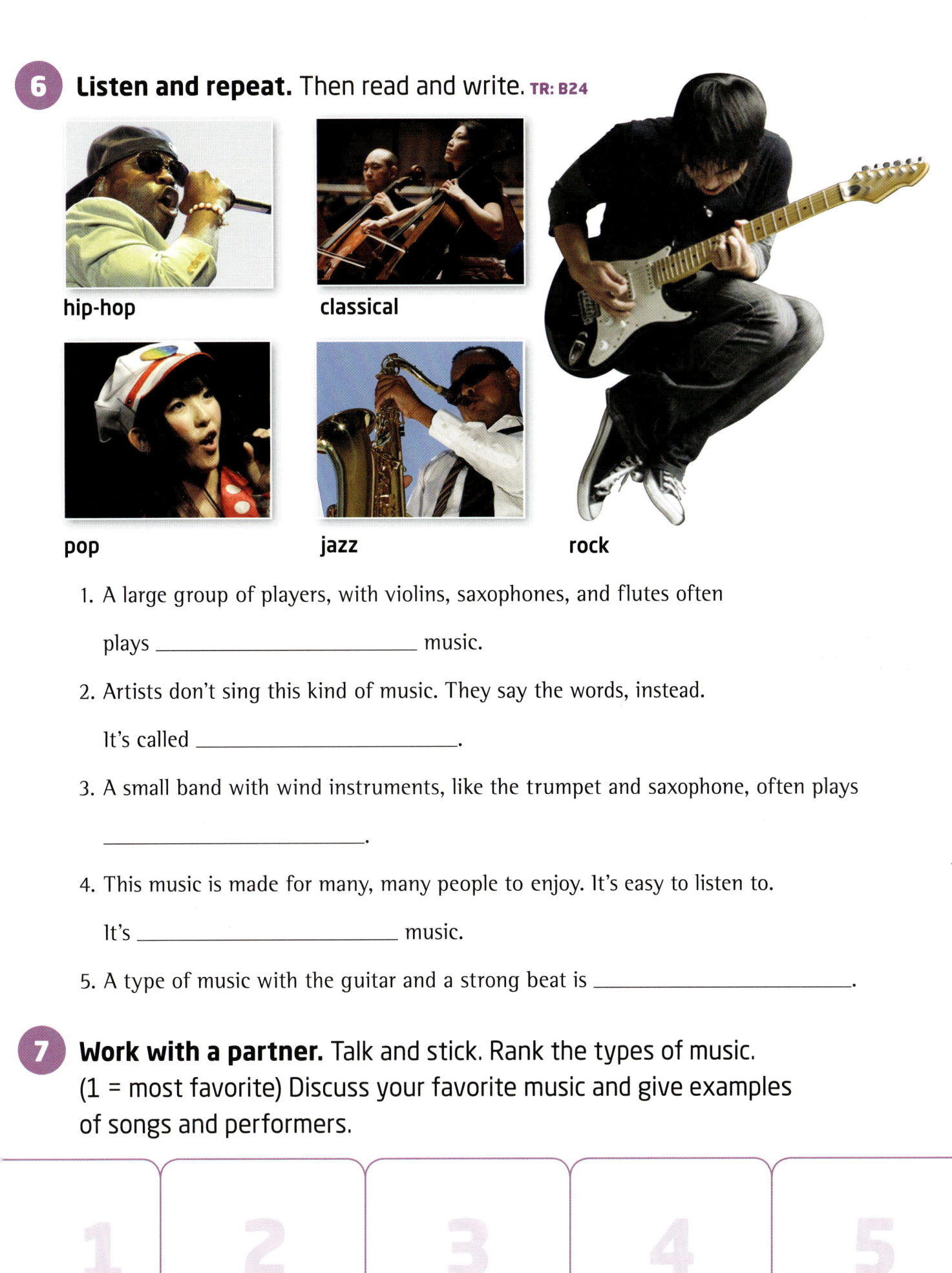

hip-hop

classical

pop

jazz

rock

1. A large group of players, with violins, saxophones, and flutes often plays _____ music.

2. Artists don't sing this kind of music. They say the words, instead. It's called _____.

3. A small band with wind instruments, like the trumpet and saxophone, often plays _____.

4. This music is made for many, many people to enjoy. It's easy to listen to. It's _____ music.

5. A type of music with the guitar and a strong beat is _____.

7 Work with a partner. Talk and stick. Rank the types of music. (1 = most favorite) Discuss your favorite music and give examples of songs and performers.

1   2   3   4   5

GRAMMAR TR: B25

He sings **more loudly than** I do.
I play the guitar **more often than** my brother.
She rides her bike **more carefully** these days.

She plays the violin **better than** he does.
He practices piano **less often than** I do.
They sing **worse than** they used to!

8 **Work with a partner.** Make comparisons. Ask and answer. Take turns.

1. Name two singers. Who sings more beautifully? Who sings more loudly?
2. Name two athletes. Who runs faster? Who wins more often?
3. Name two relatives. Who works or studies harder? Who speaks more quietly?
4. Name two types of music. Which type do you dance to better? Which do you listen to more often?

9 **Play a game.** Play with a partner. Take turns. Spin and make sentences.

He sings better than I do.

10 Listen, read, and sing. TR: B26

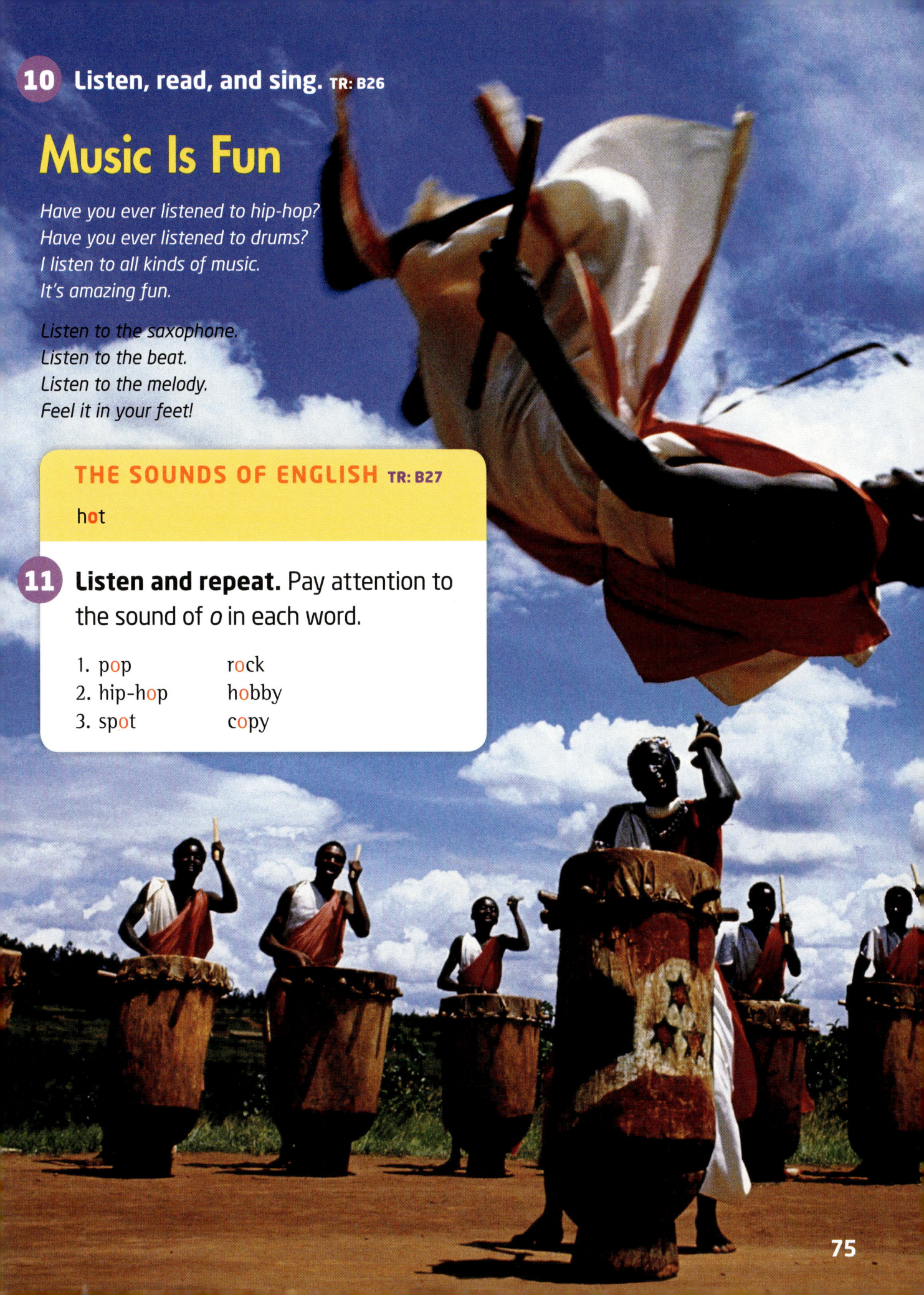

Music Is Fun

Have you ever listened to hip-hop?
Have you ever listened to drums?
I listen to all kinds of music.
It's amazing fun.

Listen to the saxophone.
Listen to the beat.
Listen to the melody.
Feel it in your feet!

THE SOUNDS OF ENGLISH TR: B27

h**o**t

11 **Listen and repeat.** Pay attention to the sound of *o* in each word.

1. p**o**p   r**o**ck
2. hip-h**o**p   h**o**bby
3. sp**o**t   c**o**py

12 **Listen and read.** TR: B28

Listen to This!

"Hey, turn that music down!"

Do you ever wonder why your parents tell you to turn the volume down when you're listening to loud music? It's not because they don't like the type of music. (Well, hip-hop *might* not be their favorite music!) It's important to listen to music and other sounds at the right volume because if you don't, it can hurt your ears!

Did you know that sound travels in waves? Sometimes, a sound is too high or too low for people to hear, depending on how fast or slow the sound waves are moving. The movement of sound can be measured in units called hertz (Hz). The range that humans can hear is 20–20,000 Hz. Dolphins can hear sounds from 75–200,000 Hz! That means they can hear things we can't.

We measure the volume of a sound in decibels (dB). The sound of people whispering is about 30 dB, the sound of a rock concert is closer to 115 dB, and the sound of a jet engine is about 140 dB! The maximum output of most MP3 players is between 70–90 dB, which is really loud! Try to keep the volume at 50 dB, or a level that allows you to easily hear people around you talking. Your ears will thank you!

Elephant	Human	Dog	Dolphin
5–10,000 Hz	20–20,000 Hz	40–60,000 Hz	75–200,000 Hz

13 **Role-play.** Imagine you have a younger brother or sister who is listening to very loud music. Tell him or her to turn down the sound and explain why very loud music is not good.

Change through music.

Has a song ever made you feel differently about something? How did the song change you?

NATIONAL GEOGRAPHIC

Jack Johnson
National Geographic Arts Ambassador for the Environment

"Music can change the world. It can inspire people to care, to do something positive, to make a difference."

Unit 8
Life Out There

Look at the photo.

1. Check the things you can see.
   - ☑ the Milky Way
   - ☐ stars
   - ☐ animals
   - ☐ mountains
   - ☐ oceans
   - ☐ light
   - ☐ umbrellas
   - ☐ jackets
   - ☐ gloves

2. How often can you see stars where you live?
   a. never
   b. sometimes
   c. every night

The Milky Way

1 **Listen and read.** TR: B29

2 **Listen and repeat.** TR: B30

Did you know that the sun is a star? Long ago, people thought that the sun traveled around our **planet**, Earth. But they were wrong! Earth **orbits** the sun. In fact, lots of planets orbit the sun! The sun and all the planets that orbit it make up one big **solar system.** Earth is not as important as we used to think!

A large group of stars, dust, and gas held together by gravity is a **galaxy.** Our galaxy is called the Milky Way. It has about 100 billion stars. That's amazing! Outside our galaxy, there are more galaxies! In fact, the **universe** is filled with galaxies. How many? We don't know! There are too many, and many are too far away to see.

an orbit

a planet

space

A **comet** is a cloud of rock, ice, and gas that orbits the sun. Many earth years pass in its **journey** around the sun. Scientists **search space** for comets. Then they predict when the next one will appear. Have you ever seen a comet?

a comet

a galaxy

Think of the many galaxies in the universe. Think of the many stars in each galaxy. Think of the many planets that orbit the stars. Do you think that **extraterrestrials** may live on one of the planets? No one knows the answer!

3 **Work with a partner.** What did you learn? Discuss.

What's the solar system?

It's the sun and all the planets that go around it.

GRAMMAR TR: B31

I **may** become an astronaut, but I'm not sure.
We **might** find life on another planet. It's possible!
It's cloudy, so you **might** not see the comet.

We **will** learn more about planets next year in school.
I'm sure we **will** find life on another planet.
You **won't** see the comet tonight. It's too cloudy.

4 **Talk to a partner.** Then check. Compare your answers.

	Right	Wrong
1. I may have a birthday next year.		✓
2. Extraterrestrials will visit our school next week.		
3. I will travel to Mars tomorrow.		
4. We might find water on other planets one day.		

> That's wrong! I will have a birthday next year. I always do!

5 **Work in groups of three.** Cut out the cards and the word box on p. 111. Explain why each thing could be useful on a hike to see a comet at night.

> We should wear warm clothes. It will be cold.

> Why don't we take some water?

> Right. We may feel thirsty.

6 **Listen and repeat.** Then read and write. TR: B32

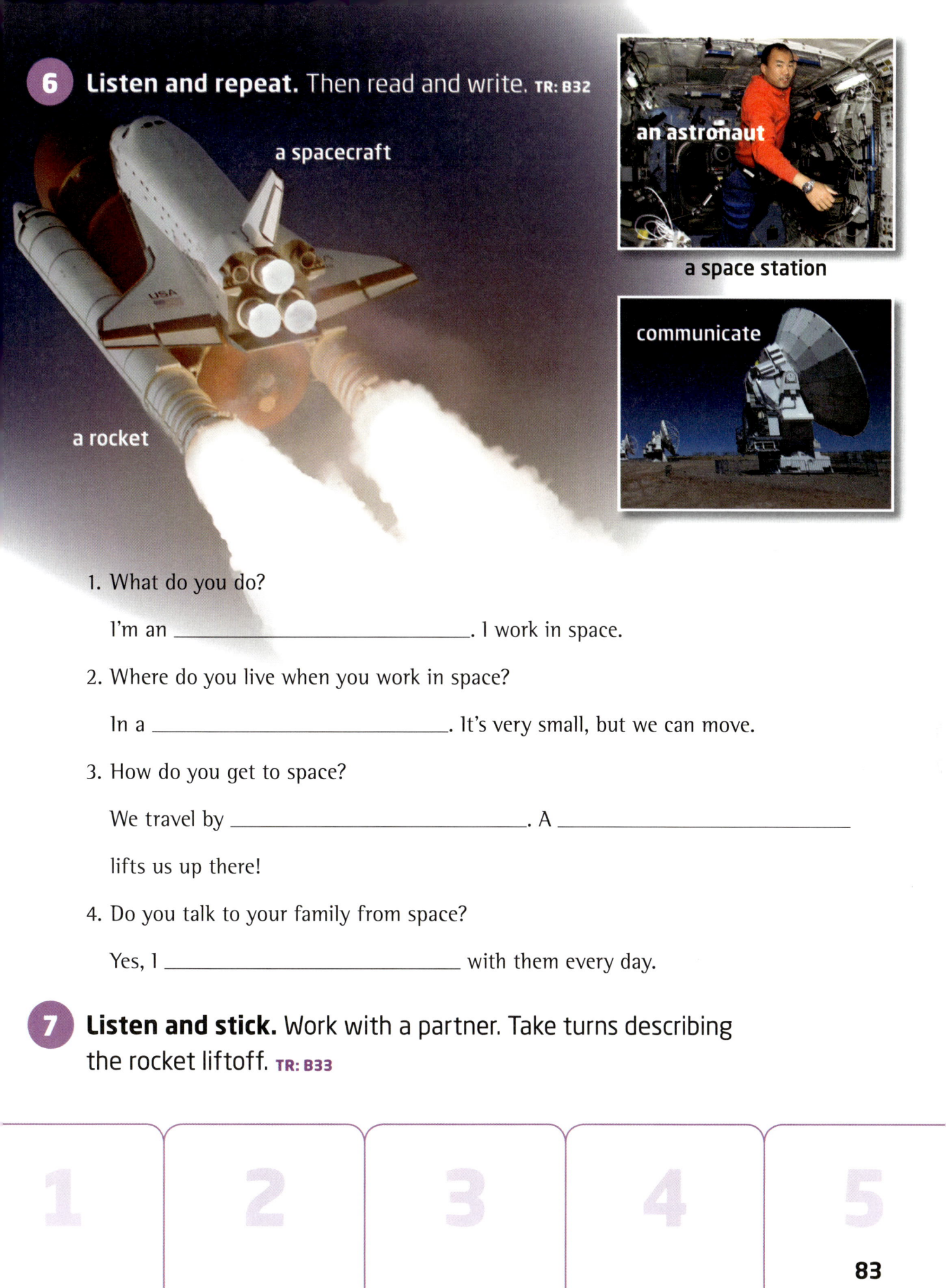

a spacecraft

an astronaut

a space station

communicate

a rocket

1. What do you do?

   I'm an _____. I work in space.

2. Where do you live when you work in space?

   In a _____. It's very small, but we can move.

3. How do you get to space?

   We travel by _____. A _____ lifts us up there!

4. Do you talk to your family from space?

   Yes, I _____ with them every day.

7 **Listen and stick.** Work with a partner. Take turns describing the rocket liftoff. TR: B33

1 2 3 4 5

83

GRAMMAR TR: B34

Did **everyone** see that comet?
Someone will go to Mars one day.

Does **anyone** want to be an astronaut?
No one can see all the stars in the universe.

8 **Read and write.** Complete the paragraph.

> anyone   everyone   no one   someone

_____ likes to think about life on other planets.

Does _____ know the answer? No!

_____ knows for sure if there is life out there or not. If _____ tells you that she knows, she really doesn't know.

9 **Work in groups of three.** Ask and answer questions. Take turns. Make notes.

1. Does anyone in this group think there is life on other planets?
2. Name one thing everyone in your family does.
3. Name a kind of music that no one in your group likes.
4. Name a funny habit someone in your family has.
5. Name someone in your class who would like to be an astronaut.

10 **Discuss.** Share the results of your survey.

> Everyone in this group thinks there's life on other planets.

11 **Listen, read, and sing.** TR: B35

Deep in Outer Space

Let's all take a journey
past the atmosphere,
beyond our solar system,
far away from here.

We might find a new planet.
We might find a new place.
We might find things we've never seen
deep in outer space.

Deep in outer space,
who knows what we might find?
Deep in outer space,
deep in outer space!

THE SOUNDS OF ENGLISH TR: B36

name

12 **Listen and say.**

1. name   never
2. astronaut   journey
3. station   dolphin

Rosette Nebula

85

13 **Listen and read.** TR: B37

Listening for Life

Have you ever seen a movie about extraterrestrials? They come to Earth and cause trouble, or they make friends with us, right? The movies are fun, but real life is very different. No one has seen an extraterrestrial. If they exist, they live on planets in other solar systems. That's very far away. Right now, we can't see the planets in other solar systems, even with our biggest telescopes.

We haven't heard from an extraterrestrial yet, either. Some people think that they are trying to communicate with us. But to do this, extraterrestrials would need to send a message through space. Their message would have to travel a long way to reach our solar system. That could take thousands of years! The signal that we receive would be very weak, so we might not hear the message. But that doesn't mean we're not listening. Scientists have set up a system of satellite dishes to search outer space for sounds of life from other planets.

One day we may know the truth about extraterrestrials. For now, let's enjoy the movies!

Weird but true The first astronauts were fruit flies. They were launched on February 20, 1947.

14 **Should we search for life?** Write why and why not.

I think it's a good idea to search for life because . . .	I think it's a bad idea to search for life because . . .

Length of time needed for radio waves to reach Earth

Earth	431 light-years	27,000 light-years	2,480,000 light-years	13,100,000,000 light-years
	North Pole star, Polaris	The center of the Milky Way	The nearest galaxy, Andromeda	As far as we can see in the universe

Be curious.

Think about things you want to know. How can you find answers?

Jupiter

Europa

NATIONAL GEOGRAPHIC

Kevin Hand
Planetary Scientist/Astrobiologist
Emerging Explorer

"We finally have the tools and technology to answer this age-old question: Are we alone? Jupiter's moon Europa is a beautiful place to go and explore that question."

Review

1 **Carla is doing a survey about music.** What are her questions? What do Laura and Andres answer? Listen. Complete the chart. TR: B38

Questions	Laura	Andres
1.	hip-hop	
2.		
3.		He likes to sing. He sang in public once.
4.	none	

2 **Do a survey.** Ask two other students the same questions. Take notes.

3 **Work in groups of three.** One of you is going on vacation to a place with extreme weather. How are you going to prepare? Take turns asking questions and giving advice.

hurricane
sandstorm
flood
ever
blizzard
never
tornado
plan
supplies

I'm going to Antarctica! That's cool, isn't it? Have you ever been there?

No, I've never been there. What are you going to pack?

I'm going to bring very warm gloves!

If you go to Antarctica, you need more than warm gloves!

4. Match the animal. Find the photo that matches the text.

frog | katydid | cheetah

1. This animal has stripes. The stripes tell predators that it is poisonous.
2. This animal has spots, which act as camouflage when it hunts other animals.
3. This animal copies the color of a leaf. It uses the leaf to hide.

5. Write. Choose 4 objects from the list. Write clues for your partner to guess. Use words from the list.

> This insect is as green as the leaf it sits on. **a katydid**

cat	cheetah	dog	drough	drum	guitar
horse	hurricane	katydid	lightning	piano	thunder
as...as	not as... as	more (quickly) than		less (often) than	

6. Work with a partner. Practice and perform a role-play.

Student A: You think there may be life on other planets.

Student B: You don't believe there is life on other planets.

| anyone | everyone | journey | no one | someone | universe |
| communicate | galaxy | may/might | planet | spacecraft | |

> I think there may be life on planets in other solar systems.

> If you are right, why doesn't anyone from other planets communicate with us?

Let's Talk

It's my turn.

I will . . .
- take turns.
- give commands.
- talk about who won a game.

1 **Listen and read.** TR: B39

Marco: **Whose turn is it?**
Amy: It's my turn.
Marco: Well, **hurry up!**

Amy: Yay, **I won!**
Marco: Now **we're tied.**
Amy: **No way.** What do you mean?
Marco: Well, I won last time!

Whose turn is it? It's my turn. It's his / her turn.	Hurry up! Come on!	I won! We're tied. Sorry, you lost!	No way. That's not true. That's not possible.

2 **Work with a partner.** Use the chart. Take turns talking about playing a game.

Who's going to take notes?

I will . . .
- talk about a classroom task.
- make a request.
- offer to do something.

3 **Listen and read.** TR: B40

Sonia: So, I'll be the reporter. **Who's going to** take notes?
Olga: **I'll do that.**
Sonia: Thanks. **Can you** watch the time, Hans?
Hans: Sure.
Hans: Um, **what page are we on?**
Olga: **We're on page** 25. We're sharing ideas about music.
Hans: Thanks, Olga.

Who's going to _____ ? Can you _____ ?	I'll do that. I'll (watch the time). I'll be _____ . I can _____ .	What page are we on? Which page is it?	We're on page _____ .
		How long do we have?	We have _____ .
		What are we doing?	We're _____ .

4 **Listen to two discussions.** Circle what the students are doing. TR: B41

1. They are a. doing a role-play.   b. doing a crossword.   c. preparing a poster.
2. They are a. doing a role-play.   b. doing a crossword.   c. preparing a poster.

5 **Work in groups of three.** Prepare and practice discussions. Choose one task. Discuss how you are going to do it.

1. Make a musical instrument from recycled objects.
2. Make a mural about copycat animals.
3. Make a poster about the weather.

Irregular Verbs

Infinitive	Simple Past	Past Participle	Infinitive	Simple Past	Past Participle
be	was/were	been	light	lit	lit
beat	beat	beaten	lose	lost	lost
become	became	become	make	made	made
begin	began	begun	meet	met	met
bend	bent	bent	pay	paid	paid
bite	bit	bitten	put	put	put
bleed	bled	bled	read	read	read
blow	blew	blown	ride	rode	ridden
break	broke	broken	ring	rang	rung
bring	brought	brought	rise	rose	risen
build	built	built	run	ran	run
buy	bought	bought	say	said	said
catch	caught	caught	see	saw	seen
choose	chose	chosen	sell	sold	sold
come	came	come	send	sent	sent
cost	cost	cost	set	set	set
cut	cut	cut	sew	sewed	sewn
dig	dug	dug	shake	shook	shaken
do	did	done	shine	shone	shone
draw	drew	drawn	show	showed	shown
drink	drank	drunk	shut	shut	shut
drive	drove	driven	sing	sang	sung
eat	ate	eaten	sink	sank	sunk
fall	fell	fallen	sit	sat	sat
feed	fed	fed	sleep	slept	slept
feel	felt	felt	slide	slid	slid
fight	fought	fought	speak	spoke	spoken
find	found	found	spend	spent	spent
fly	flew	flown	spin	spun	spun
forget	forgot	forgotten	stand	stood	stood
forgive	forgave	forgiven	steal	stole	stolen
freeze	froze	frozen	stick	stuck	stuck
get	got	gotten	sting	stung	stung
give	gave	given	stink	stank	stunk
go	went	gone	sweep	swept	swept
grow	grew	grown	swim	swam	swum
hang	hung	hung	swing	swung	swung
have	had	had	take	took	taken
hear	heard	heard	teach	taught	taught
hide	hid	hidden	tear	tore	torn
hit	hit	hit	tell	told	told
hold	held	held	think	thought	thought
hurt	hurt	hurt	throw	threw	thrown
keep	kept	kept	understand	understood	understood
know	knew	known	wake up	woke up	woken up
leave	left	left	wear	wore	worn
lend	lent	lent	win	won	won
let	let	let	write	wrote	written
lie	lay	lain			

Unit 1 Protect the Seas TR: A8

Please, please protect the seas.
Put good deeds into motion.
Help save the oceans.

CHORUS

We must protect
the wonders of the seas,
to make a better world
for you and me.

We must stop polluting
the ocean blue.
An octopus would like that,
and so would you.

CHORUS

We must protect
the wonders of the seas,
to make a better world
for you and me.

When we make a mess,
we can't dump it in the sea.
Sharks don't want that.
Do we?

There are layers in the
ocean below.
There are creatures there
that we don't know.
They live deep underwater.
They don't breathe air,
but our world is a part of
theirs.

CHORUS

Unit 2 Inventions TR: A18

Creativity!
Electricity!
Creativity changes the world!

Inventions solve problems.
Problems that we used to have are gone!
The wheel and the cell phone
help to make our world go around!

Inventions are useful,
every day, in every way.
Computers, cars, and airplanes
help to make our world go around.

CHORUS

You used to have to walk
to get from place to place.
Years ago, you could only talk
face to face.

You could take only boats
to get across the sea.
Now, we fly across the sky.
Inventions are the reason why.

CHORUS

Imagination and ideas
can change the world, every day.
Can you solve a problem?
Can you help our world today?

CHORUS

Unit 3 What's Your Hobby? TR: A26

What's your hobby?
What do you like to do?
What's your hobby?
I have a hobby, too!

The boy who has the highest score
wins the video game.
The girl who collects a fossil
wants to learn its name.
Who enjoys a comic book?
Who likes to compete?
I collect stuffed animals
because I think they're sweet.

CHORUS

The boy who takes a photo
sees it on the screen.
The girl who reads about dinosaurs
can see them in her dreams.
Do you like to cooperate?
Do you like to work alone?
I like to talk about my hobby
on my new cell phone.

It's fun to be creative and show what you
 can do.
Collect, compete, cooperate.
I have a hobby.
Do you?

CHORUS

Unit 4 I'm on the Move! TR: A35

Push it! Pull it! Push it! Pull it!
 Push! Pull!
Push! Pull! Push! Pull! Watch
 it go!

If you spin around, and
 around and around and
 around,
what you feel is force.
If you fall down, down, down,
 down,
down to the ground,
that's gravity, of course.

I'm on the move.
I'm in the groove.
It's amazing what you
 can do
when you let force do the
 work for you!

The more you push, the
 faster some things go.
When you spin around, the
 force comes and goes.

CHORUS

The more you push, the
 faster some things go.
When you spin around, the
 force comes and goes.

Push it! Pull it! Push it! Pull
 it! Push! Pull!
Push! Pull! Push! Pull! Watch
 it go!

If you spin around, and
 around and around and
 around,
what you feel is force.
If you fall down, down,
 down, down,
down to the ground,
that's gravity, of course.

CHORUS

I'm on the move!

Unit 5 Bad Weather TR: B8

There's bad weather on the way!
There's bad weather on the way!

Is it going to storm? Yes, it is!
Is there going to be lightning? Yes, there is!
Is there going to be thunder? Yes, there is!

When there's going to be a storm, I hurry inside!

Be prepared for emergencies.
It's always good to be safe. You'll see!
Grab supplies and a flashlight, too.
Seek shelter. It's the safe thing to do!

Is there going to be a blizzard? Yes, there is!
Is there going to be an ice storm? Yes, there is!
Is it going to be cold? Oh, yes, it is!

If there's going to be a blizzard, I hurry inside!

CHORUS

Is there going to be a hurricane? Yes, there is!
Is the wind going to howl? Yes, it is!
Are the waves going to rage? Yes, they are!

If there's going to be a hurricane, we evacuate!

Be prepared for emergencies.
It's always good to be safe. You'll see!
Grab supplies and a flashlight, too.
Seek shelter. It's the safe thing to do!
Seek shelter. It's the safe thing to do!

Unit 6 It's a Wild World TR: B18

It's a wild world!
It's work to stay alive!
Animals do amazing things
in order to survive.

An insect that looks like a leaf
copies plants to get relief.
Predators are everywhere,
and looking for a feast!

CHORUS

Camouflage and imitate.
Resemble and escape!
Animals hide in front of our eyes, every day.

The hunter and the hunted,
predator and prey,
must hunt or hide to stay alive,
each and every day.

A pretty frog can be as deadly as a snake.
Its stripes tell its enemies
"You'd better stay away!"

CHORUS

It's a wild world!

Unit 7 Music Is Fun TR: B26

Have you ever listened to hip-hop?
Have you ever listened to drums?
I listen to all kinds of music.
It's amazing fun.

Listen to the saxophone.
Listen to the beat.
Listen to the melody.
Feel it in your feet!

The flute is playing.
The piano is, too.
I can hear the guitar.
Can you?

CHORUS

Listen to the rhythm.
Listen to that band!
Sing the notes (*la la la*)
and clap your hands.

Have you ever played a note?
Have you ever played a chord?
Have you ever played a rhythm?
1, 2, 3, 4!

CHORUS

Unit 8 Deep in Outer Space TR: B35

Let's all take a journey
past the atmosphere,
beyond our solar system,
far away from here.

We might find a new planet.
We might find a new place.
We might find things we've never seen
deep in outer space.

Deep in outer space,
who knows what we might find?
Deep in outer space,
deep in outer space!

Somewhere in the universe
we might find a moon
where flowers grow.
You never know,
but I wish we'd get there soon!

CHORUS

But right here on planet Earth
life is all around.
Our world is full of color,
texture, light, and sound.

We can take a journey
right outside our door
and see the wonder of life on Earth
and so much more!

CHORUS

Deep in outer space.

| Your friend threw a plastic bag in the sea. What will happen to it? | You're going to bed very late. How will you feel tomorrow? | You left garbage on the beach. Where will it go? |

| There is an oil spill in the ocean. What will happen to the animals? | You have to do a lot of homework tonight. What time will you go to bed? | We must stop pollution. What will you do? |

| You didn't clean your bedroom. Will your parents be angry? | You throw food in the sea. Why will it disappear? | Your homework was very good. What will your teacher do? |

| How old will you be on your next birthday? How will you celebrate? | | |

Unit 2 Cutouts Use with Activity 5 on page 18.

tell the time	travel	read at night
spend free time	buy vegetables	cross the ocean
write	erase writing	make calls
ride	go to school	cook

99

Unit 3 Cutouts Use with Activity 9 on page 30.

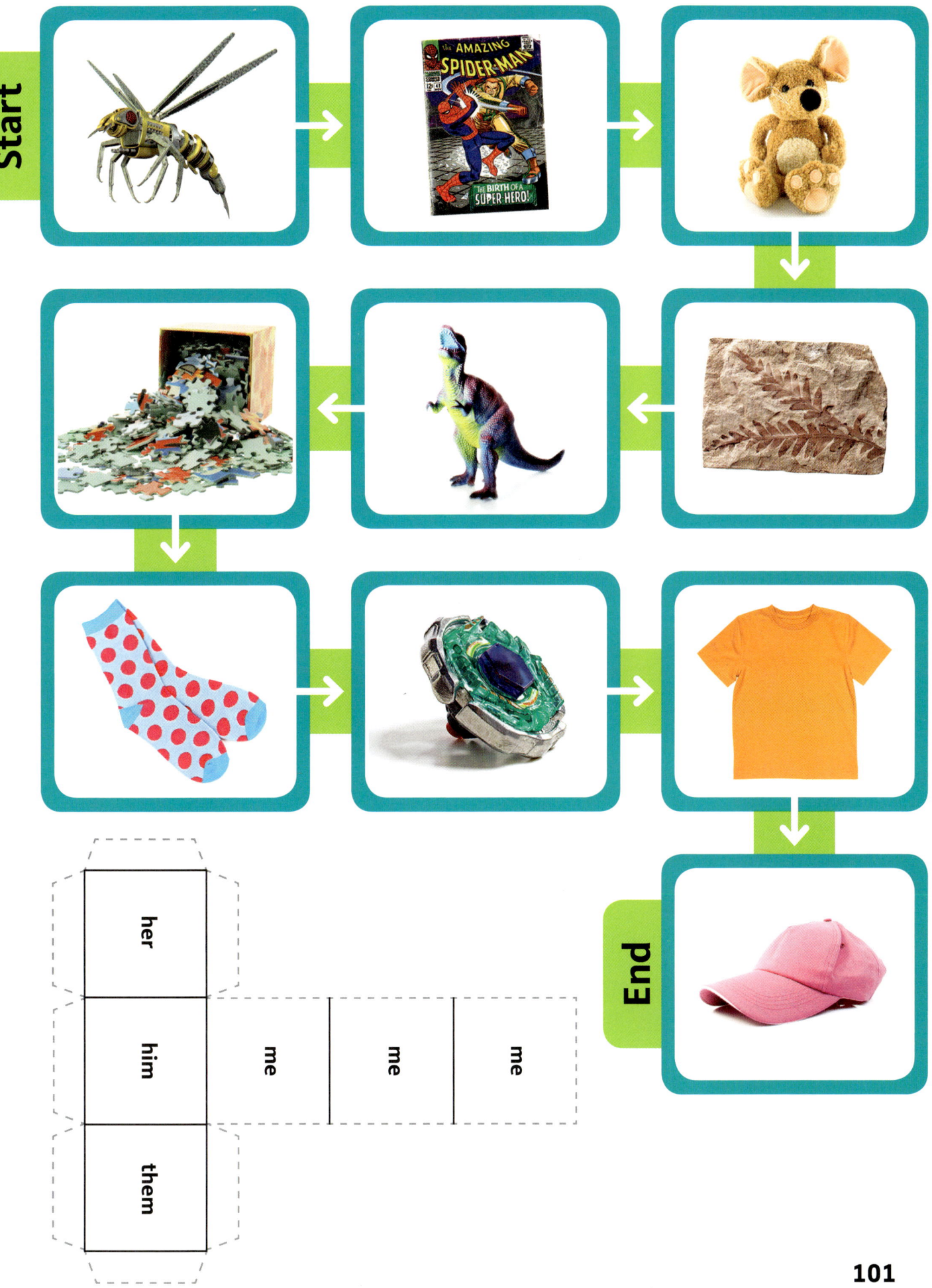

her
him
them

me | me | me

Unit 4 Cutouts Use with Activity 9 on page 40.

12

What is a bicycle? (a machine / wheels and handlebars / which / ride)

19

This is a force which pulls you to the earth. What is it?

10

Act out: pull

16

What is a skateboard? (a board with wheels / which / move on)

4

This is a playground object which goes up and down. What is it?

14

Act out: spin

24

Act out: push

Unit 5 Cutouts Use with Activity 9 on page 54.

105

Unit 6 Cutouts Use with Activity 4 on page 62.

Group A

A horse	A lion
A hippo	A crocodile
A deer	A squid

Group B

B jaguar	B alligator
B elephant	B cat
B donkey	B octopus

Use with Activity 8 on page 64.

isn't it?	is it?	aren't they?	are they?
don't they?	do they?	doesn't it?	does it?
were they?	weren't they?	did it?	didn't it?

107

Unit 7 Cutouts Use with Activity 5 on page 72.

- sing / in the shower
- listen to / a song on the Internet
- watch / a band
- learn / all the words of a song
- play / a musical instrument
- go / concert
- hear / Brazilian music
- see / a famous singer
- take / music lessons
- listen to / the radio
- buy / music
- meet / a famous person

START

FINISH

109

Unit 8 Cutouts Use with Activity 5 on page 82.

1 some cookies	2 a camera	3 warm clothes	4 raincoats
5 some water	6 a flashlight	7 boots	8 a first-aid kit
9 a cell phone	10 a gift	11 a map	12 a paper bag

hard ground	be cold	feel thirsty	fall or cut ourselves
take photos	get lost	in the dark	need to call someone
need to take our trash home	rain	feel hungry	meet an extraterrestrial!

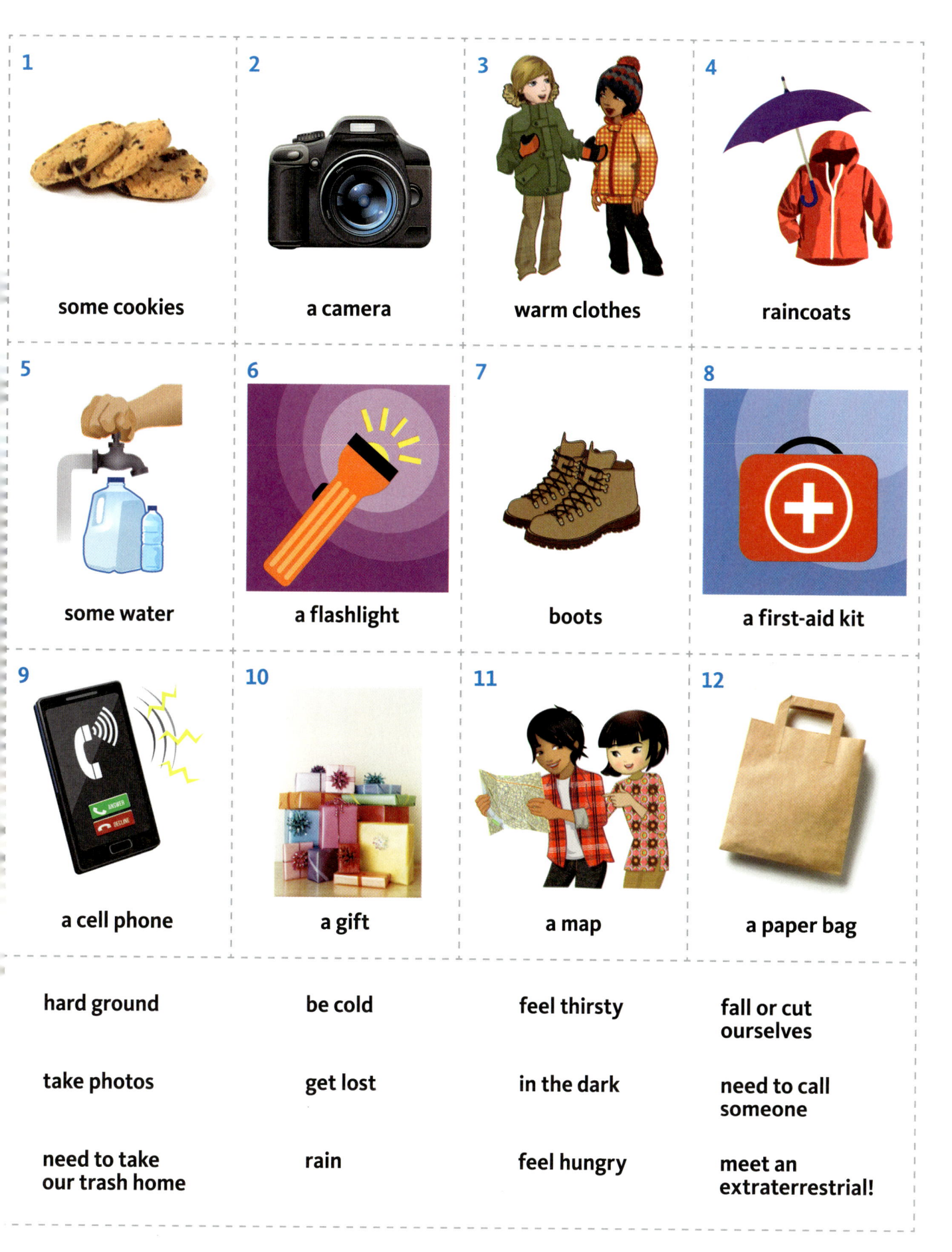

111

Unit 1 stickers

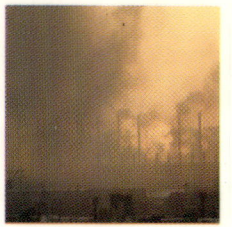

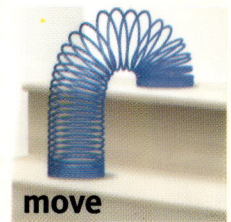

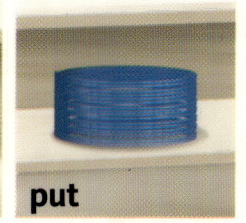

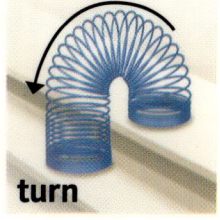

Unit 2 stickers

| move | lift | put | turn | use |

Unit 3 stickers

Unit 4 stickers

| toward | direction | push | lean | gravity |

| balance | away from |

Unit 5 stickers

Unit 6 stickers

TRUE	TRUE	TRUE	TRUE	TRUE
FALSE	FALSE	FALSE	FALSE	FALSE

Unit 7 stickers

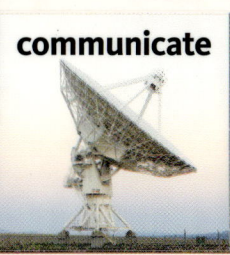

Unit 8 stickers

rocket — space station — communicate — spacecraft — astronaut